CONTENTS

The 2009 Midwest League
Championship Trophy

CHAPTER 1

OPENING DAY: April 16, 2009

After 18 months of construction, it was here.

Thursday, April 16, 2009: Opening Day at Parkview Field. The TinCaps, who won all six games on their season-opening road trip, were as perfect as the weather. It was 65 degrees outside and sunny ... In mid-April ... In Northeast Indiana.

You might have thought you were dreaming, but the Air National Guard's F-16 fighter planes rumbling overhead during an impeccably-timed fly-over would've woken you up. And so would a roaring crowd of 8,208 when James Darnell cracked a line drive over the left-field wall for a two-run home run, the first TinCaps hit at Parkview Field.

By the time the TinCaps closed out a 7-0 win over the Dayton Dragons, it was apparent that Opening Night at Parkview Field went about as well as anyone could have hoped. What nobody could have realized was that this was just the first of many memorable nights at Parkview Field in 2009.

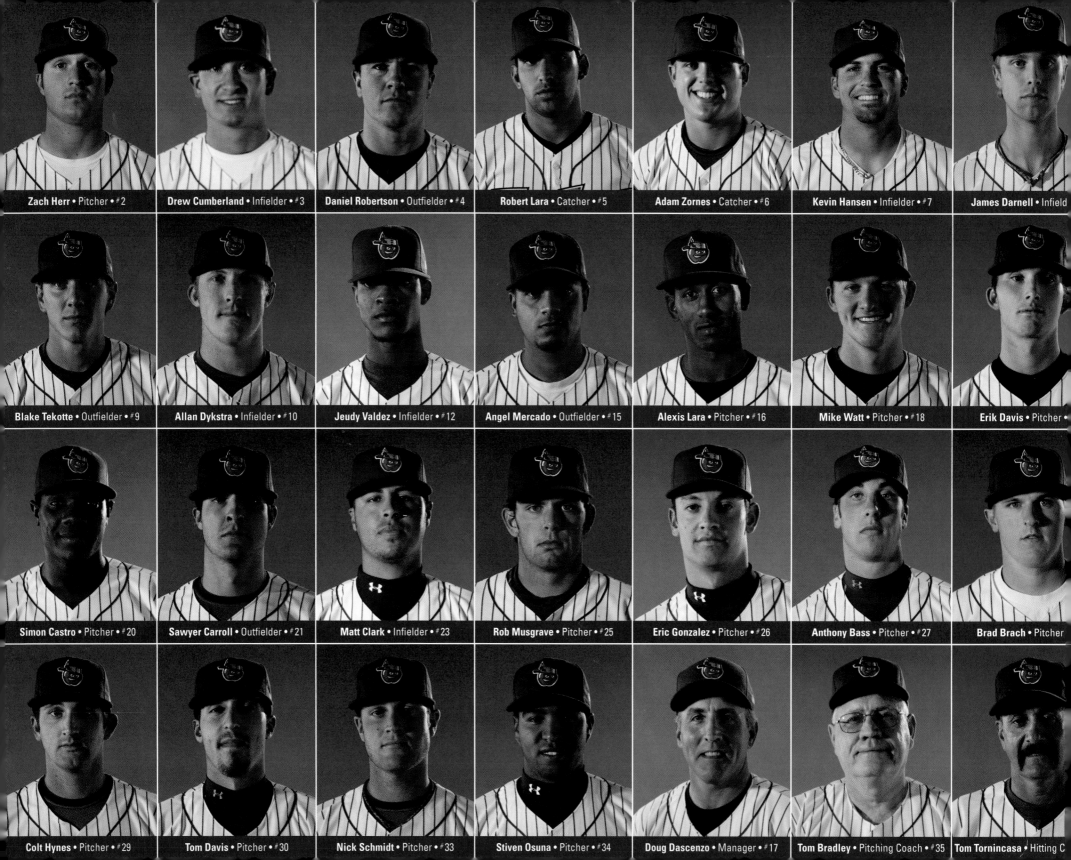

Zach Herr • Pitcher • #2

Drew Cumberland • Infielder • #3

Daniel Robertson • Outfielder • #4

Robert Lara • Catcher • #5

Adam Zornes • Catcher • #6

Kevin Hansen • Infielder • #7

James Darnell • Infield

Blake Tekotte • Outfielder • #9

Allan Dykstra • Infielder • #10

Jeudy Valdez • Infielder • #12

Angel Mercado • Outfielder • #15

Alexis Lara • Pitcher • #16

Mike Watt • Pitcher • #18

Erik Davis • Pitcher

Simon Castro • Pitcher • #20

Sawyer Carroll • Outfielder • #21

Matt Clark • Infielder • #23

Rob Musgrave • Pitcher • #25

Eric Gonzalez • Pitcher • #26

Anthony Bass • Pitcher • #27

Brad Brach • Pitcher

Colt Hynes • Pitcher • #29

Tom Davis • Pitcher • #30

Nick Schmidt • Pitcher • #33

Stiven Osuna • Pitcher • #34

Doug Dascenzo • Manager • #17

Tom Bradley • Pitching Coach • #35

Tom Tornincasa • Hitting C

Commemorative Opening Day baseballs ready to be distributed.
OPPOSITE: The Fort Wayne TinCaps Opening Day roster.

TinCaps taking batting practice.

OPPOSITE: Parkview Field was full of activity even before the gates opened with media coverage and last-minute preparations.

Jake Patton throws out a ceremonial first pitch. Jake's dad, Travis, submitted the name Fort Wayne TinCaps.

Players warm up before the game.

OPPOSITE LEFT: Mayor Tom Henry addresses the sellout crowd.

OPPOSITE UPPER RIGHT: Parkview Health CEO, Mike Packnett, welcomes fans to Parkview Field.

The Indiana Air National Guard 122d Fighter Wing presented the colors while the Voices of Unity Choir sang the National Anthem. The pre-game events culminated with an F-16 fly-over by the 122d Fighter Wing, also known as the Blacksnakes.

Here's Johnny! The TinCaps mascot made his debut on Opening Day at Parkview Field.

CHAPTER 2

THE FIRST HALF

Entering 2009 the Fort Wayne franchise had never won more than eight games in a row. The TinCaps won their first ten games, four by shutout. Following two months of back-and-forth in first place with West Michigan, on June 17 the TinCaps pummeled the Whitecaps 12-2 to clinch Fort Wayne's first playoff birth since 2006. Four days later, the TinCaps clinched the first-half Eastern Division championship, the first for Fort Wayne since 2003. The TinCaps finished the first half with a 45-25 record, shattering the franchise record of 41 wins in a half.

The first half saw many standout performances. Outfielder Jaff Decker joined the club two weeks into the season after recovering from a spring training concussion; the 19-year-old clubbed a home run in his first at-bat with the TinCaps and never slowed down. Right-handed pitcher Mat Latos gave up only one run in 25 innings before being promoted. Two months later, he became the first player to pitch in Fort Wayne and make his Major League Debut in the same season, as Latos won four of his first five Major League starts with the San Diego Padres.

Five TinCaps—third-baseman James Darnell, outfielder Sawyer Carroll and pitchers Brad Brach, Anthony Bass and Zach Herr—were selected for the Midwest League All-Star Game in June. Carroll, who went 4-for-4, was named the MVP of the mid-summer classic in Clinton, Iowa. The first half would be a tough act to follow, but the TinCaps were primed for the challenge.

OPPOSITE: Infielder Jeudy Valdez shatters his bat during early season action. 17

Drew Cumberland picks out uniform pants before a pre-season workout.

OPPOSITE: Once suited up, Cumberland took batting practice at Parkview Field for the first time.

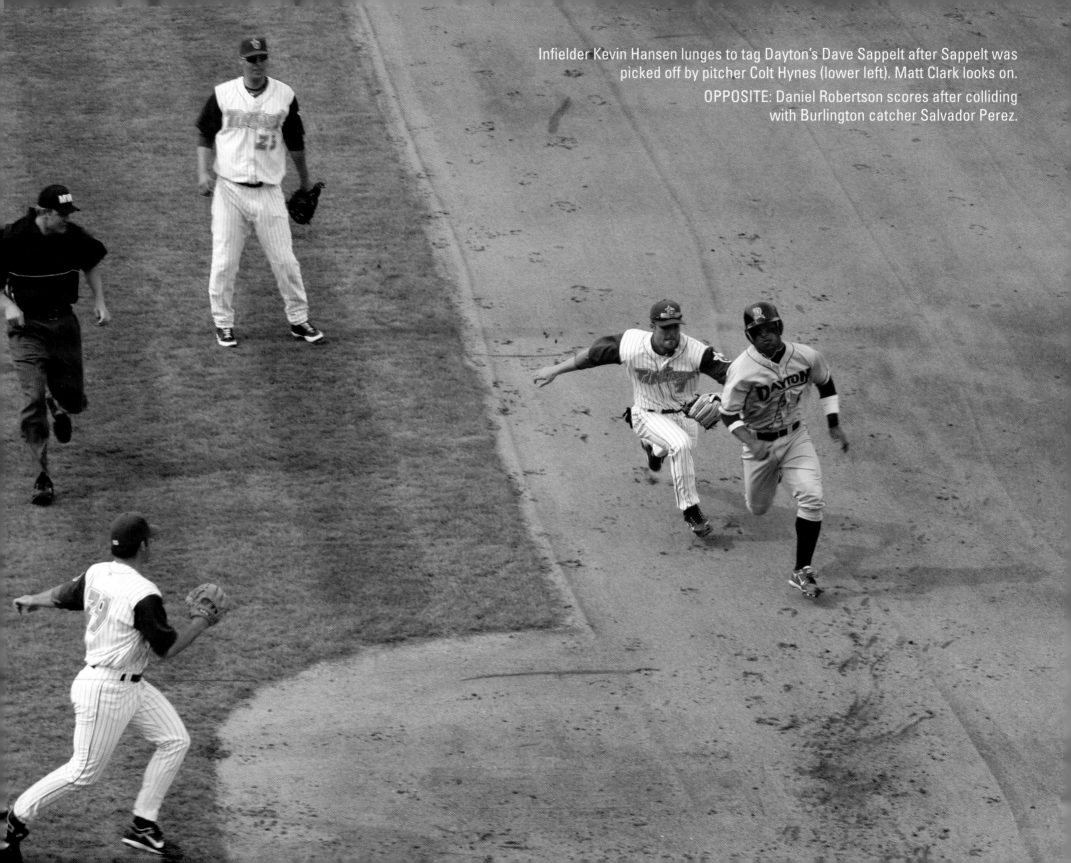

Infielder Kevin Hansen lunges to tag Dayton's Dave Sappelt after Sappelt was picked off by pitcher Colt Hynes (lower left). Matt Clark looks on.

OPPOSITE: Daniel Robertson scores after colliding with Burlington catcher Salvador Perez.

TinCaps third baseman James Darnell takes a swing.
OPPOSITE: Robert Lara collects his thoughts in the dugout.

CHAPTER 3

ENTERTAINMENT

Parkview Field proved to be a special place, and not just because of home runs, strikeouts and diving catches.

Where else would you see four adults dressed as hamburger buns trying to "build a burger?"

Where else could you watch as a t-shirt was shot out of a cannon 250 feet across the outfield?

Where else would a 65-year-old man's dance moves be shown on a gigantic video board… to thunderous applause?

Speaking of dance moves… what about those Bad Apple Dancers?

And how in the heck did QuickChange switch their clothes so fast?
And where did the clothes go?

Yep, Parkview Field became the place for fun on summer nights in Fort Wayne, whether you love baseball or just like seeing the ridiculousness surrounding the game.

They're not your average grounds crew.
The Bad Apple Dancers strut their stuff at the end of the 6th inning.

Harry Canary of the ZOOperstars entertains the crowd.
OPPOSITE: BirdZerk shakes his tail feathers with a fan.

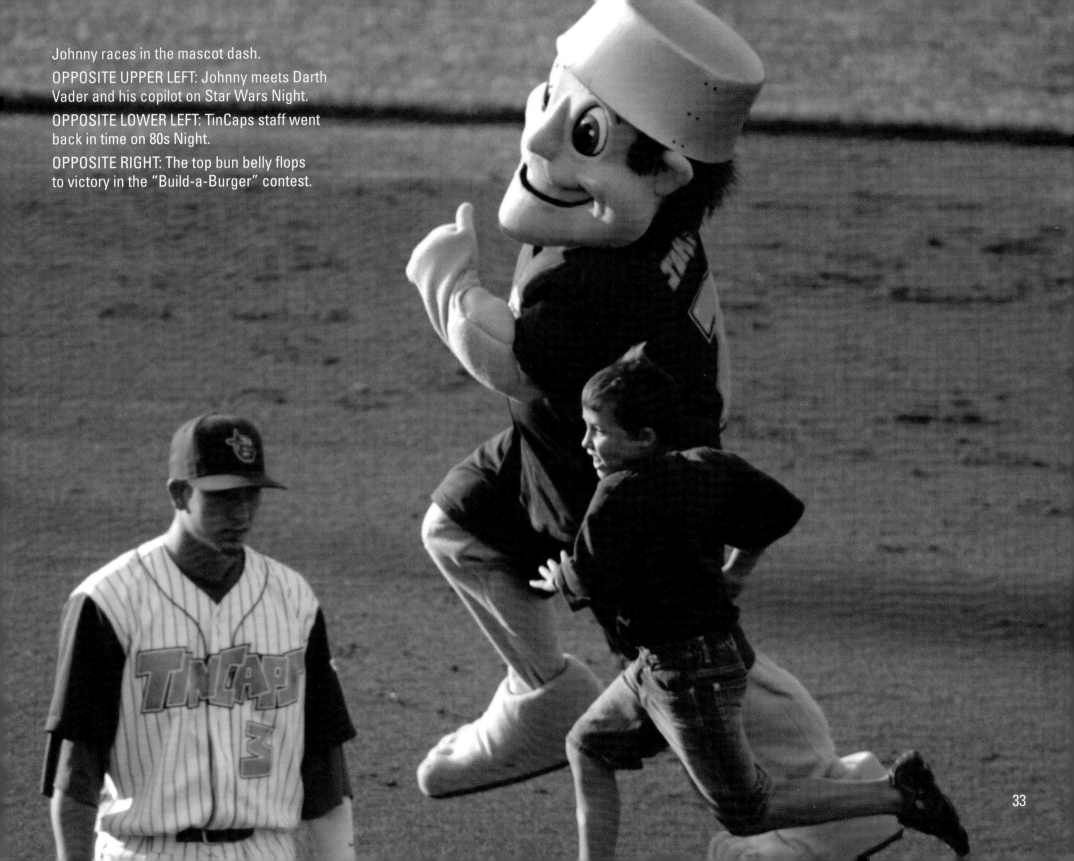

Johnny races in the mascot dash.

OPPOSITE UPPER LEFT: Johnny meets Darth Vader and his copilot on Star Wars Night.

OPPOSITE LOWER LEFT: TinCaps staff went back in time on 80s Night.

OPPOSITE RIGHT: The top bun belly flops to victory in the "Build-a-Burger" contest.

CHAPTER 4

THE SECOND HALF

After a historic first half, player promotions were inevitable. Opening Day starting pitcher Nick Schmidt and heart of the batting order (infielders Matt Clark and James Darnell and outfielder Sawyer Carroll) were promoted to Advanced-A Lake Elsinore at the All-Star break. Conventional wisdom said the TinCaps would struggle in the second half.

Conventional wisdom was wrong.

The TinCaps bolted out to a 23-4 start in the second half, building a seven-game cushion on the nearest competitor by the end of July. When ace pitcher Anthony Bass was promoted, Simon Castro stepped up to anchor the starting rotation. Castro pitched a seven-inning no-hitter on August 18 against Dayton, the first no-hitter in franchise history.

The offense seemed to have a different hero each game. Fort Wayne topped its own franchise record by winning 49 games in the second half, winning the Eastern Division by eight games. The TinCaps' 94 wins in the regular season were the most in Minor League Baseball since 2003 and the most in the Midwest League in 22 years.

OPPOSITE: Erik Davis went 11-3 with a 3.01 ERA in the second half.

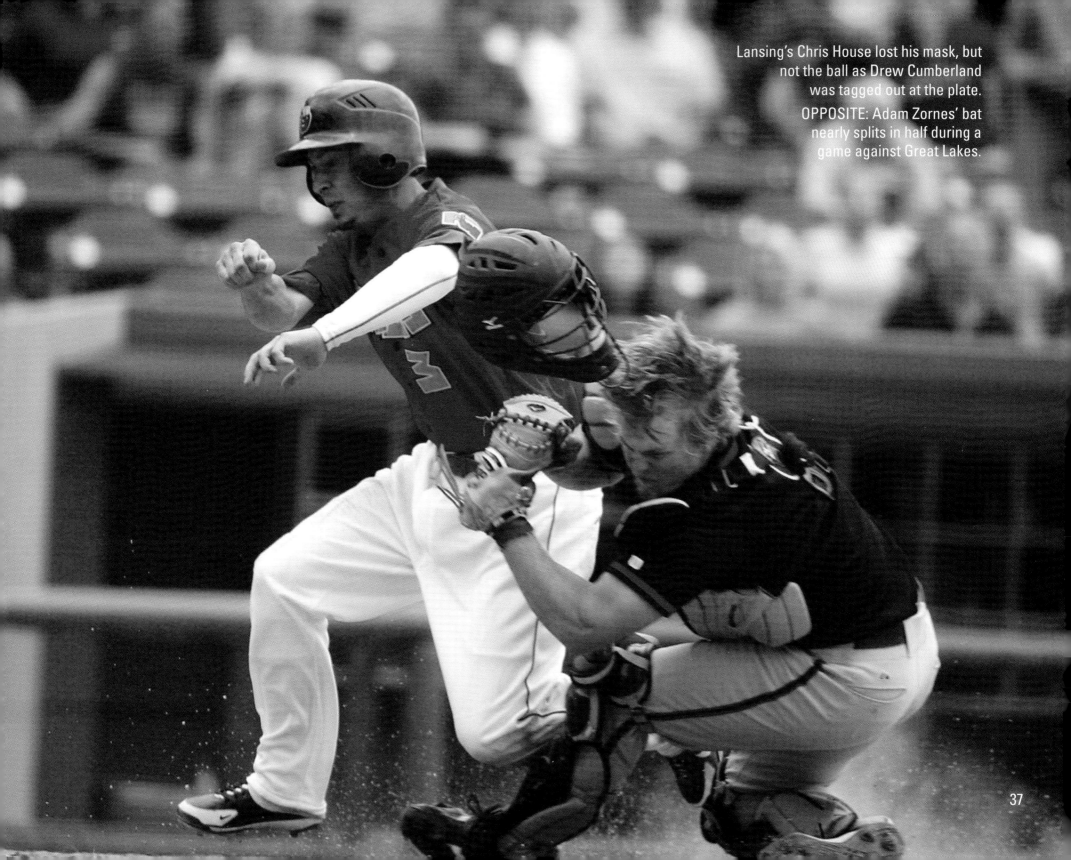

Lansing's Chris House lost his mask, but not the ball as Drew Cumberland was tagged out at the plate.

OPPOSITE: Adam Zornes' bat nearly splits in half during a game against Great Lakes.

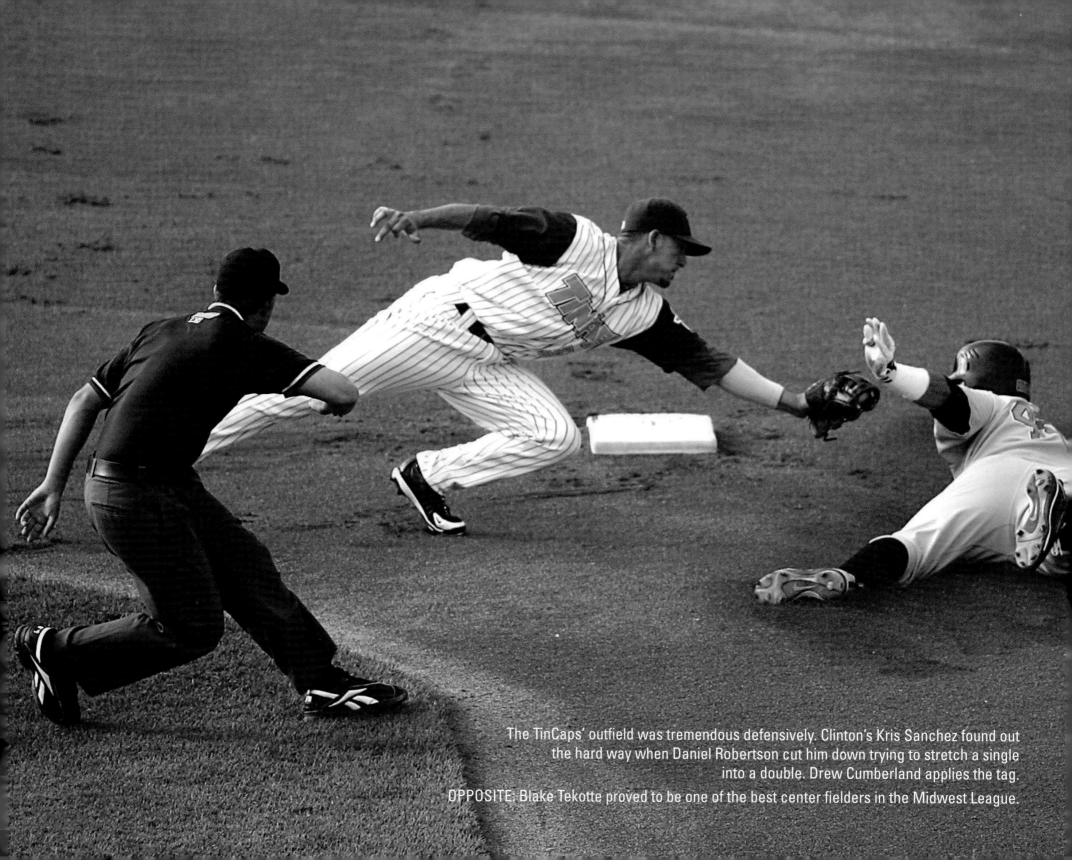

The TinCaps' outfield was tremendous defensively. Clinton's Kris Sanchez found out the hard way when Daniel Robertson cut him down trying to stretch a single into a double. Drew Cumberland applies the tag.
OPPOSITE: Blake Tekotte proved to be one of the best center fielders in the Midwest League.

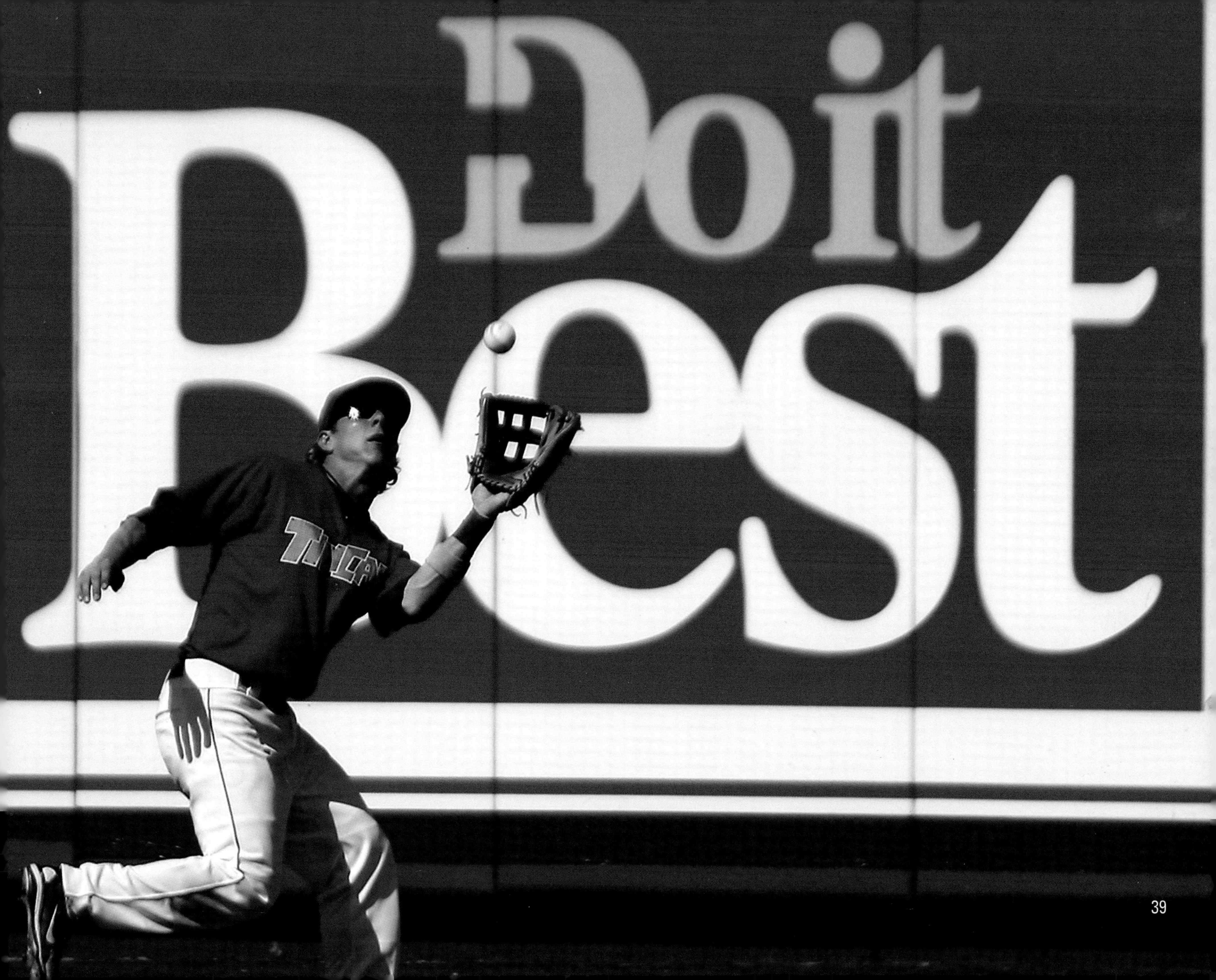
Do it
Best

On August 23rd against Lansing, Blake Tekotte led off the bottom of the 13th inning with a game-winning home run. It was the first time a game at Parkview Field ended with a home run.

OPPOSITE: Nick Schumacher loosens up in the bullpen.

Simon Castro threw Fort Wayne's first no-hitter on August 18th (a seven-inning game) versus the Dayton Dragons.

43

CHAPTER 5

TINCAPS MANIA: The Fans at Parkview Field

They came, they saw, they wore foam pots on their heads. Yes, these were the TinCaps' fans in 2009, and they came to Parkview Field in droves. In fact, the 378,529 fans who came through the turnstiles, during the regular season alone, set a franchise attendance record.

They didn't just show up and sit on their hands, either. Manager Doug Dascenzo alluded to home games feeling like "rock concerts" with the fans energizing the TinCaps and intimidating the opponent. That's what you call a home-field advantage.

OPPOSITE: Kevin Hansen bats as a packed house looks on.

Pitcher Dexter Carter signs autographs following a Sunday afternoon game.
OPPOSITE: Fans fill the TinCaps team store.

51

CHAPTER 6

MIDWEST LEAGUE CHAMPIONS

If you had sent the TinCaps' playoff script to Hollywood, it would have been rejected. Everybody's already seen this movie... Overly dramatic comeback from unlikely sources, team wins a championship, perfect ending. Too predictable. But it happened.

Down by a run with two outs in the bottom of the 8th against South Bend in the decisive game of the first round of the playoffs, Cole Figueroa slashed a two-run double into the left field corner, providing the TinCaps with a dramatic one-run victory.

In the Eastern Division Championship series, a loaded Great Lakes Loons team came from behind four different times to defeat the TinCaps in Game 1. A return to the friendly confines of Parkview Field led to a 9-4 victory in Game 2, setting the stage for what one reporter called "the greatest moment in Fort Wayne Professional Baseball History."

Game 3. A win means a trip to the Championship and a loss ends the season. The TinCaps overcome 2-1 and 3-2 deficits in the seventh and eighth to send the game into extra innings tied 3-3. In the bottom of the 10th, catcher Robert Lara came to the plate. He didn't have a single hit in 15 post-season at-bats. He hadn't hit a home run in more than two months. Lara quickly got behind in the count. On the ninth pitch of the at-bat, after working the count full, Lara cracked a long drive to left-center. That's right, a game winning home-run from the player who hadn't had a hit in over a week and had only two homers the entire season. And it sent the TinCaps to the championship series for the first time in franchise history. (The mob scene at home plate is pictured at left).

From there, the TinCaps rattled off three straight victories over the Burlington Bees to sweep the Midwest League Championship. You could've made a movie about it. But no one would have believed it.

2009 MIDWEST LEAGUE PLAYOFFS

First Round
(Best-of-3 series)

Fort Wayne 3 • South Bend 1
South Bend 12 • Fort Wayne 7
South Bend 4 • **Fort Wayne 5**

Eastern Division Championship
(Best-of-3 series)

Fort Wayne 10 • **Great Lakes 11**
Great Lakes 4 • **Fort Wayne 9**
Great Lakes 3 • **Fort Wayne 4**

Midwest League Championship
(Best-of-5 series)

Burlington 2 • **Fort Wayne 6**
Burlington 0 • **Fort Wayne 2**
Fort Wayne 4 • Burlington 3

Infielder Cole Figueroa hit a team-best .406 in the playoffs, including this clutch go-ahead two-run double with two outs in the bottom of the 8th in the decisive game against South Bend on September 11th. The TinCaps beat the Silver Hawks (5-4) to advance to the Eastern Division Championship Series.

Pitcher Chris Fetter watches the TinCaps TV broadcast while icing his arm.
OPPOSITE: Robert Lara, Brad Brach, and Alexis Lara celebrate on the mound after the TinCaps' 5-4 comeback win over South Bend.

Pitching coach Tom Bradley discusses strategy with Fetter, Catcher Robert Lara, and first baseman Allan Dykstra.

OPPOSITE: Chris Fetter provided the TinCaps with two strong starts during the post-season.

Robert Lara's walk-off series-winning home run against Great Lakes on September 14th sent Parkview Field into pandemonium.

Robert Lara takes a curtain call after his dramatic home run against Great Lakes.

OPPOSITE: Justin Baum steals second ahead of the tag of Burlington's Fernando Garcia. Baum shrugged off a shoulder injury to hit .364 with eight RBIs in six post-season games.

Chris Fetter unleashes a pitch during the TinCaps' final home playoff game, September 16th against Burlington. He fired 5.1 scoreless innings in a 2-0 win.

OPPOSITE: Pitch Dexter Carter used unique tactics while urging the TinCaps to victory.

Manager Doug Dascenzo meets with the media during a post-game interview on September 16th. The TinCaps had just taken a 2-0 lead with their victory over Burlington.

OPPOSITE: The fans at Parkview Field give the team a standing ovation, while TinCap Daniel Robertson thanks the fans.

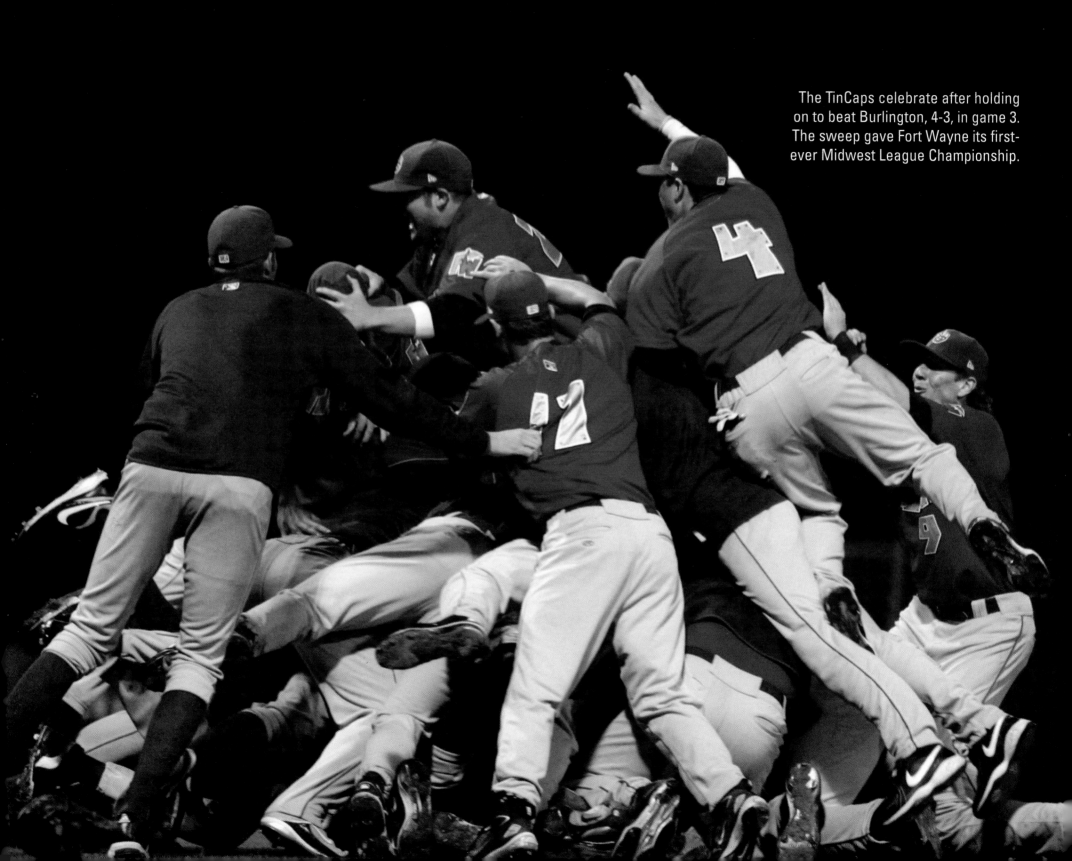

The TinCaps celebrate after holding on to beat Burlington, 4-3, in game 3. The sweep gave Fort Wayne its first-ever Midwest League Championship.

The TinCaps relive their championship moment on the big screen at Parkview Field.

OPPOSITE: Doug Dascenzo addresses the fans. Johnny shows off the championship trophy. Robert Lara signs autographs.

CHAPTER 7

THE CONSTRUCTION OF PARKVIEW FIELD

From an under-utilized piece of downtown property, local builders created what started as a large hole in the ground but was to become "the most innovative minor-league ballpark in America." With expectations high and temperatures often low, work continued over 18 months, leading right up to Opening Day.

In September 2008, Parkview Health stepped up as the naming rights partner and this state-of-the art facility became known as Parkview Field. The partnership quickly proved to be more than just a name. Parkview Health brought is expertise to the ballpark with healthy food options at the concessions stands and health screenings for fans. This dynamic relationship will benefit the Fort Wayne community for years to come.

Less than a month later, the team itself was renamed; the Wizards became the TinCaps in a nod to Johnny Appleseed, the frontier hero who lived in Fort Wayne. Uniforms were unveiled in December. The front-office staff moved downtown in February 2009. Later that month, the video board (all 1,400 square feet of it) made its premiere. But would anybody show up?

A resounding "yes" came on February 26th, when Opening Day tickets sold out 27 minutes after going on sale. That was only the beginning of selling out Parkview Field with 19 standing room only crowds during the regular season. When the dust settled after the Midwest League Championship over 400,000 fans had attended a TinCaps game during the 2009 storybook season.

OPPOSITE: Parkview Field's immaculate field was installed October 2008.

Harrison Square, as the construction footprint was originally called, was just a blank canvas as demolition had been completed and construction was about to get underway in earnest.

OPPOSITE: The steel framework went up quickly for the ballpark.

OPPOSITE BOTTOM RIGHT: The player tunnel entrance took shape as the concrete was poured for the dugout and seating areas.

On September 11, 2008 Parkview Health, Fort Wayne TinCaps, and the City of Fort Wayne announced the naming of Parkview Field. Mayor Tom Henry (right) and Parkview CEO Mike Packnett (below) made the announcement to the media standing on what would become home plate.

Starting clockwise above:
The concrete work for the centerfield splash pad and amphitheater.
The main seating area concrete forms are positioned into place.
Giant styrofoam blocks are positioned under the outfield lawn areas.
Sod is put into place on the outfield berms weeks before Opening Day.

81

The backstop screen is installed. The field is covered with a growth blanket to encourage root growth.
OPPOSITE: Rolls of sod and loads of dirt are delivered to Parkview Field to complete the playing surface.

The centerfield concourse bar, grill and restrooms take shape.
OPPOSITE LEFT: The 1,400 square-foot videoboard is installed.
OPPOSITE RIGHT: The field lights at Parkview Field are turned on for the first time.

The south gate at Parkview Field takes shape during construction.

CHAPTER 8

EXTRA INNINGS

Baseball is a collector's dream. Significant seasons, games and individual moments can be remembered with bats, balls, ticket stubs, scorecards and more. There were plenty of reasons to remember the 2009 season. The most significant item, the Midwest League Championship trophy, holds the names of the TinCap players that contributed to the championship season. The TinCaps have also chosen to recognize the efforts of the TinCaps front office by including their names on the trophy as well. Below are how the names appear on the 2009 Midwest League Championship trophy.

Manager - Doug Dascenzo
Hitting Coach - Tom Tornincasa • Pitching Coach - Tom Bradley
Trainer - Dan Turner • Strength & Conditioning Coach - Mark Brennan

Dean Anna • Anthony Bass • Justin Baum • Vince Belnome
Brad Brach • Sawyer Carroll • Dexter Carter • Yefri Carvajal
Simon Castro • Matt Clark • Jason Codiroli • Drew Cumberland
James Darnell • Erik Davis • Cody Decker • Jaff Decker • Brayden Drake
Allan Dykstra • Chris Fetter • Cole Figueroa • Eric Gonzalez
Nick Greenwood • Kevin Hansen • Zach Herr • Colt Hynes • Alexis Lara
Robert Lara • Mat Latos • Colin Lynch • Rob Musgrave • Stiven Osuna
Eduardo Perez • Daniel Robertson • Nick Schmidt • Nick Schumacher
Blake Tekotte • Jeudy Valdez • Mike Watt • Adam Zornes

Jason Freier • Chris Schoen
Mike Nutter • David Lorenz • Brian Schackow • Michael Limmer
Jared Parcell • Brad Shank • Justin Shurley • Brent Harring • Tyler Baker • Ryan Ledman
Patrick Ventura • Chris Snyder • Tony DesPlaines • Allan Wertheimer • Abby Naas • Dan Watson
Karen Schieber • Cathy Tinney • Tim Burkhart • Chris Watson • Mitch McClary • Grant Bodkin
Bill Lehn • Jenn Bales • Scott Kammerer • Holly Raney • Barbara A'Hearn

OPPOSITE: Pitcher Zach Herr enjoys a sunset from the bullpen.

With 227 wins, Doug Dascenzo finished 2009 with the most victories (regular and post-season) by a manager in Fort Wayne franchise history. He was voted the Midwest League's Co-Manager of the Year.

Pitcher Mat Latos went 3-0 with a 0.36 ERA for the TinCaps. After a promotion to Double-A San Antonio, he was chosen to play in the Futures Game, part of the All-Star festivities at Busch Stadium in St. Louis. On July 19, just two months after leaving Fort Wayne, Latos made his Major League debut with the Padres, winning 4 of his first 5 starts.

Outfielder Jaff Decker hit .299 and led the TinCaps with 16 home runs despite being one of the youngest players in the league at age 19. He also led the full-season minor leagues with a .442 on-base percentage. Following the season, Decker was named the Class-A Player of the Year by *Baseball America*.

RECORDS ARE MADE TO BE BROKEN

A multitude of records went by the wayside during the 2009 season. Off the field, the front-office staff got into the act, winning the Midwest League President's Trophy, among others. Wins, walks, whatever else you could think of, the 2009 TinCaps did it better than any team Fort Wayne has ever seen.

REGULAR SEASON RECORDS	Previous Record	New Record
Longest Win Streak	8 (2003)	10 (two times)
Longest Home Win Streak	8 (1998)	15
Wins at Home	47 (1998)	50
Wins in Regular Season	79 (1998)	94 (101 with playoffs)
Wins in Half	41 (1998)	49
Team Shutouts, Pitching	16 (1993)	18
Team Walks, Offense	571 (1999)	681
Team Home Runs	93 (2005)	97
Team RBIs	650 (1998)	661
Team Strikeouts, Pitching	1,185 (2004)	1,224
Fewest Errors	156 (2006)	130
Individual Walks	80 (John Scheschuk - 2000)	104 (Allan Dykstra)
Individual Wins	15 (LaTroy Hawkins - 1993)	16 (Erik Davis)
Low Ind. ERA, min. 45IP	1.33 (JJ Trujillo - 2000)	1.11 (Nick Schumacher)
Career Wins, Manager	209 (Randy Ready)	220 (Doug Dascenzo)
Attendance, Season	318,506 (1993)	378,529 (404,318 with playoffs)
Attendance, Single Game	7,760 (2002)	8,572
Attendance, Playoff Game	2,379 (9/3/95)	6,269 (9/16/09)

The ball **Jaff Decker** hit over 450 ft onto the right field Treetops party area.

The ball that recorded the **final out** of the 2009 Midwest League Championship.

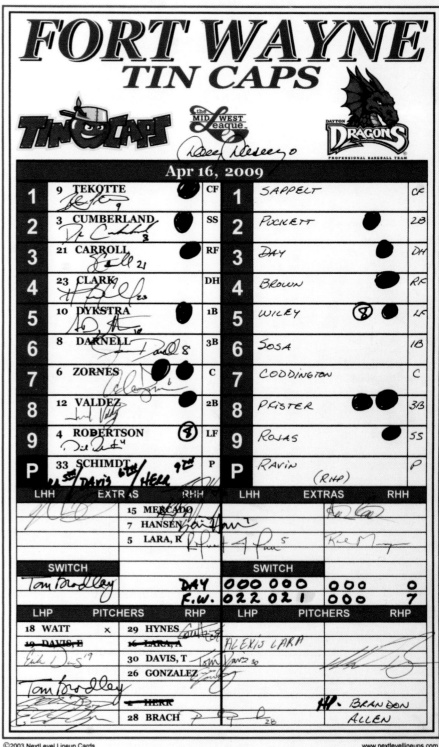

Doug Dascenzo's lineup card from Opening Day signed by each player.

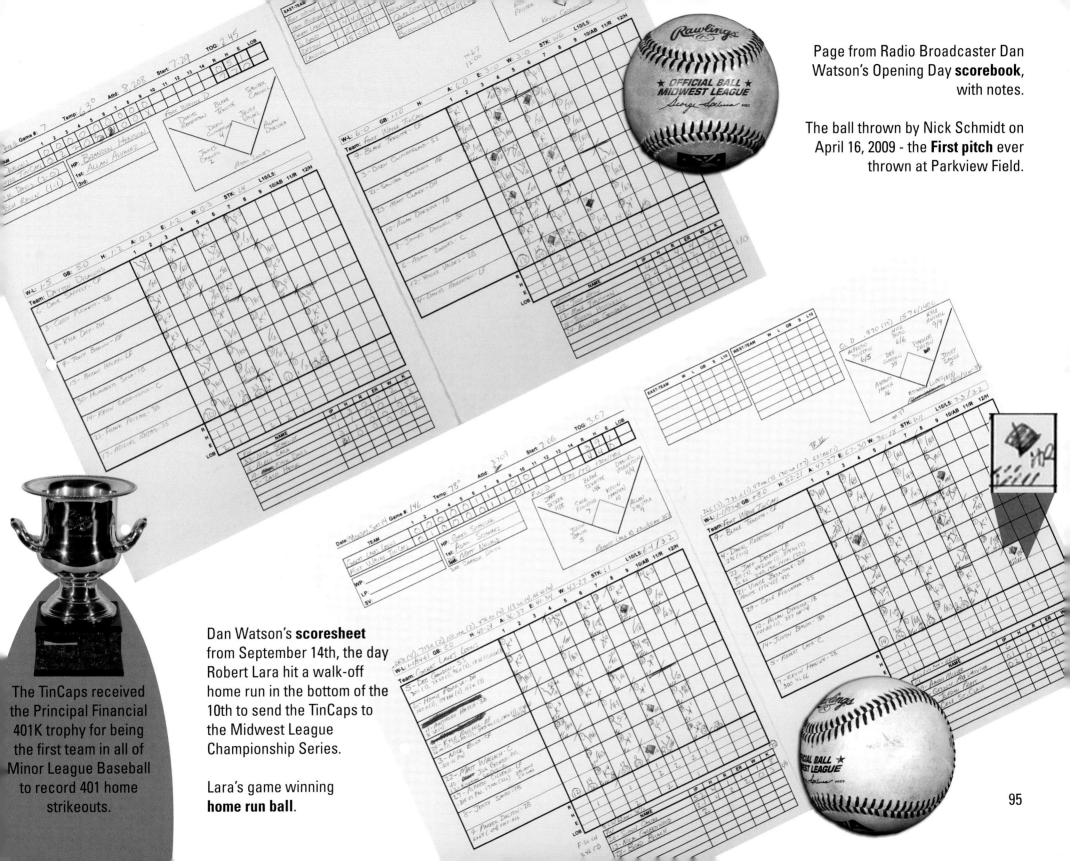

Page from Radio Broadcaster Dan Watson's Opening Day **scorebook**, with notes.

The ball thrown by Nick Schmidt on April 16, 2009 - the **First pitch** ever thrown at Parkview Field.

The TinCaps received the Principal Financial 401K trophy for being the first team in all of Minor League Baseball to record 401 home strikeouts.

Dan Watson's **scoresheet** from September 14th, the day Robert Lara hit a walk-off home run in the bottom of the 10th to send the TinCaps to the Midwest League Championship Series.

Lara's game winning **home run ball**.

PHOTOGRAPHY